The Virus Poems

Mike Bourton
and his dog Bruce

To Sam
M?x

Author/Illustrator: Mike Bourton
Copyright Poems and Pictures Ltd 2020
The moral right of the author/illustrator has been asserted

A CIP catalogues record of the publication is available from the British
Library.

ISBN: 9781916254282

Publisher: Poems and Pictures Ltd www.poemsandpicturespublishing.org
Designer: Jack Bourton
Printed in the UK

www.theviruspoems.com

POEMS & PICTURES
—— PUBLISHING ——

The Covid-19 virus outbreak of 2020 will forever be a pivotal part of human history. The impact was global and affected everyone on the planet. Here, in the UK, we managed the coronavirus in similar ways to other countries but also with a degree of Britishness that has defined us for centuries. Not that it was all good and it raised many issues about our culture and values.

This is not the time to write about statistics – you can look that up yourself. However, hundreds of thousands caught the virus and many thousands died. The impact on the nation, on families and our very own NHS was palpable and at times, almost too much to bear.

In my local town, a Facebook group was set up to help people, to communicate and provide support to anyone that might need it. It became incredibly important for many and it was here that I started writing 'The Virus Poems'. A friend, knowing that I wrote, suggested I should post one on the site to spread a little observational humour and comment. That began the journey that ended 67 days later on the 31st May 2020.

When you read just one poem it might touch you or amuse you. It is when you consider every subject that, without knowing, this has become a walk through our time in 'Lockdown' as this period will be forever known.

I have also included alongside every poem an extract of the news headlines of the day to help you put the poems into some context. But enjoy them and the illustrations in any way you wish.

I must also provide a huge thanks to some key people who helped along the way. My friend, Susanne, who first suggested writing, my sister Helen, who got to read each poem before anyone, and my son, Jack, who put this book together.

There is also one last mention that I have great delight in including – my dog, Bruce. He has been an inspiration, a wonderful adoring canine partner who has transformed my life. Enjoy!

Contents

26th March 2020

I came back from working abroad and to my astonishment, suddenly the shops were emptying of toilet rolls and paracetamol. So it was an easy start for the subject of this first virus poem.

News headlines

The Prince of Wales has tested positive for coronavirus, Clarence House has announced. Prince Charles, 71, is displaying mild symptoms "but otherwise remains in good health", a spokesman said, adding that the Duchess of Cornwall, 72, has been tested but does not have the virus. Charles and Camilla are now self-isolating at Balmoral. Buckingham Palace said the Queen last saw her son, the heir to the throne, on 12 March, but was "in good health". The palace added that the Duke of Edinburgh was not present at that meeting, and that the Queen was now "following all the appropriate advice with regard to her welfare".

The hoarder on the run

I sit here with my toilet roll and wonder what I've done
I could tell by the look on the cashier's face, 'You're a hoarder on the run'.

I've only got 104 left, I counted them last night.
So, it's just as well I bought some more. I can't risk it, right?

Fortunately, my pasta stock is filling the spare room.
So only need a few bags more to save myself from doom.

'Wash your hands' the people said. 'Clean germs you mustn't get',
You must be mad I can't do that; it will spoil my lovely set.

Of sanitisers big and small, every brand and make I've got,
Next to my bags of headache pills, I think I've got the lot.

Now I must watch the daily news, to check what's running out,
And barge to the front of the shopping queue. Just a hoarder not a lout.

So, if you see me running in the street with my shopping bags undone.
Please don't chase me anymore, I'm a hoarder on the run.

I can't help it, I need help and an extra government loan.
So, I can buy my lovely things to fill my bulging home.

Spare a thought at these difficult times for lonely people like me.
I can't help it, I really can't, now has anyone some tea.

Oh, there's a thought - must go and get some more!

27th March 2020

So, we have now started our lockdown and are having to adjust to what we can and cannot do. This might be difficult to achieve and cope with, but time will tell.

News headlines

Prime Minister Boris Johnson has tested positive for coronavirus and is self-isolating in Downing Street. He said he had experienced mild symptoms over the past 24 hours, including a temperature and cough, but would continue to lead the government. England's Health Secretary Matt Hancock said he had also tested positive while England's Chief Medical Officer, Prof Chris Whitty, has shown symptoms.

Social distance rules

Gosh this is really complicated, this 'social distancing'.
I've ordered a ruler from amazon, a flexible folding thing.

Then when I'm out walking my dog, I can wave it in the air.
Don't come too close and hit my rule, not if you really care.

I did think about making something, that I could strap across my head,
Then I realised it would be a pain, so got the ruler instead.

Now I'm also still confused, about things I'm allowed to do,
If I exercise in the supermarket, does that count as one or two?

Times I'm allowed outside my flat to venture forth alone.
Or must I keep it separate from the policeman's secret drone.

I'm sure there's one up watching us, up in the skies above.
Of course, it not as obvious. Its disguised as a big grey dove.

So, 7 days or 14, inside my little flat.
I marked it up on a chart on my fridge, just 10 more days, that's that!

Until then I'm a good boy and do what I've been told,
By Boris and his faithful team. Doesn't he look old!

He's got so much upon his plate, but I bet he's not like me.
Still waiting for my ruler and my delayed delivery

Maybe I should phone them one more time.

28th March 2020

I really was walking my dog in the evening to avoid the crowds and my sister rang me to talk about it – I had completely missed the first Clapping. I suspect there will be more to come.

News headlines

The government has asked local authorities in England to house all rough sleepers and those sleeping in hostels and night shelters by the weekend, as part of efforts to contain the spread of coronavirus. The Ministry of Housing said: "We are all redoubling our efforts to do what we possibly can at this stage to ensure that everybody is inside and safe by this weekend, and we stand with you in this."

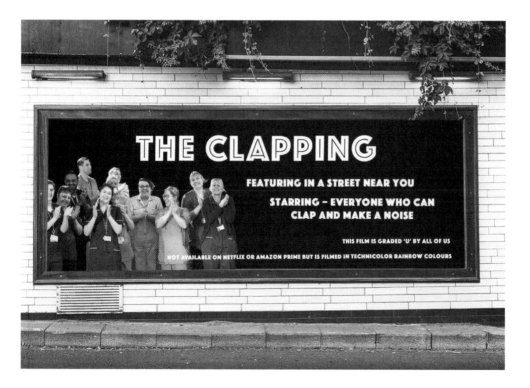

The Clapping

Somehow, I missed the clapping. I found out too late.
My flat has no one near it, as I reached my little gate.

To walk the dog down the High Street. I couldn't hear a thing.
I really missed the moment, to hear the people sing.

Then I got the messages, 'What do you think of that?'
'Think of what' I messaged back, wondering what was at.

Do I pretend that I was there, and shed a little tear?
For our lovely NHS and how we want to care.

Well thank god for timing, I haven't missed a thing.
We're doing it again next week so please give me a ring.

To remind me to warm my digits and bang my frying pan.
Then I'll be outside doing it, doing all I can.

So, excuse me for missing, I must be the only one.
I'll double up my clapping, for our healthy evensong.

Sorry

29th March 2020

It seems ironic that our PM has contracted the virus – but maybe it will help drive the message home to the population that it does not discriminate at all. He seems indestructible.

News headlines

Britain must stay in total lockdown until June to properly prevent the full extent of the deadly coronavirus and social distancing could last for months, a senior health chief has warned. Professor Neil Ferguson, the government's leading epidemiology adviser, said Britons would have to remain in their homes for nearly three months. The Prime Minister, who is self-isolating after testing positive for Covid-19, said on Saturday 'things will get worse before they get better' as he stressed the need to stay indoors to support the NHS by slowing the spread.

Boris

I feel sorry for Boris and hope he soon is back.
To quote his normal turn of phrase, he 'will get back on track'.

I know I'm not the only one, who sees another man.
A politician from way back, who ruled as Boris can.

Its Churchill that I see in him, only with more hair.
He's almost got the voice as well, just no planes in the air.

And so, the 'few' are nurses to get our Boris well.
Working day and night for us. Oh, and Doctors ring that bell.

Now back to Boris, I've had another thought,
And this is about his messy hair, not the battles that he's fought.

Ok he hasn't got a beard, like his 'best friend', Jeremy!
But now he's got a real excuse to let his hair go free.

He can't go to the hairdresser to comb his golden locks.
He'll probably have a ponytail, or a mullet - that will rock!

Imagine him in briefing with rock star hanging hair.
Will you still believe him, when he says, 'we're nearly there?'

Back on track!

30th March 2020

It didn't initially register on my radar that it would be difficult to get hold of food for my dog Bruce. Then, as the Amazon order hadn't arrived, I realised I had to think of new options. Fortunately, a local pet shop came to the rescue – but what if they had been unable to help.

News headlines

It could be six months before life in the UK returns to "normal", England's deputy chief medical officer has said. Speaking at the government's daily coronavirus briefing, Dr Jenny Harries added: "This is not to say we would be in complete lockdown for six months." But, she continued, the UK had to be "responsible" in its actions and reduce social distancing measures " gradually".

No food for my dog

I've run out of dog food, so what do I give him?
I don't know what his preferences are. Where do I begin?

Not too hot and spicy, that's obvious, obviously.
Can't give human chocolate, that's because it's all for me.

So, don't think he can have potatoes, although I'm sure he would.
The way he gobbles things that fall and barks 'that's jolly good'.

Don't be silly, he can't talk. It would be good if he did.
Then I could ask him if he likes, 'Sunny eggs or flipped'.

Definitely no onions, or citrus fruit, I think.
Mind you given half a chance; he'd eat the bloody sink!

Do I do pudding too, or 'afters' if you're posh.
Not sure if he would like it, just a plate of nosh.

Well I guess it could be worse, he could be cooking too.
All the food in the same bowl, no cutlery for you.

And now I think about it, it doesn't seem quite fair.
I eat on my table and he eats right down there.

And so, I've laid for dinner, a dinner just for two.
With candles, napkins, cruet set and a thoughtful inked menu.

Didn't turn out like I planned; it was over really quick.
Wolfed it down in seconds, with a final juicy lick.

No morale with this story, just pondering out loud.
Next time buy more dog food, as much as your allowed

Can you pass the salt Bruce?

31st March 2020

With very few cars on the road, some have taken the opportunity to start using the roads to drive around at speed and at night. The street outside my flat sometimes sounds like a racetrack. I wonder where they are going.

News headlines

Frontline doctors have reported they have been gagged from speaking out about shortages of protective equipment as they treat coronavirus patients – with some claiming managers have threatened their careers. Staff have been warned not to make any comments about shortages on social media, as well as avoiding talking to journalists, while NHS England has taken over the media operations for many NHS hospitals and staff.

An essential key worker

I'm an essential key worker, I need to drive my car.
I need to play my music loud and I need to drive it far.

So, officer, please let me go and send me on my way.
I promise I will go straight home, that's me all done today.

Strange thing he didn't buy it and now I have a fine.
How am I supposed to pay that? It's surely not a crime!

To drive around and check the shops, the ones with lots of stuff.
And no one there to stop me, until I've got enough!

That's right I'm an essential key worker. I steal to pay my bills.
The government needs to support me, I've a lock up garage to fill.

So now I'm ploughing through the forms, I'm self-employed you see.
Can I get my 80%, of the things I steal for me?

I'm an essential key worker, I work all through the night.
So, officer, please let me work, you surely know it's right.

Can I make my phone call now please?

1st April 2020

It was inevitable that I would make I sure I had enough of some basic food items during my self-isolation. And so, it came to pass – overindulgence in insuring I had enough beans!

News headlines

Britons have been warned of the potential for blackouts amid fears that staff shortages could lead to issues with the country's power network.Fears have been raised that staff sickness during the coronavirus outbreak, mixed with the government's self-isolation rules, could lead to a shortage of engineers. The National Grid insists that the network is able to cope, while industry chiefs have described it as 'one of the most reliable networks in the world'.

The Beans

Things are getting desperate now, I'm smoothying baked beans.
And of course, that's using up my rolls, if you know what I mean.

Just how many ways can you use them, clearly on toast is the best.
But roasting them ain't working and let me share the rest.

I've tried them in a salad and mixed with cottage cheese.
I've plonked them on a pork pie but now I'm on my knees.

One more baked potato with baked beans on the top,
Would be ok with cheese as well, but my dog ate the flipping lot.

Beans with fettuccine might sound posh for you,
But I'm running out of patience and running to the loo!

I wonder if I could fry them and turn them into jam.
So, jam sarnies and bean cake too. I'm mad that's what I am.

I begin to wish I chosen more, instead of baked bean packs.
But only got a few tins left and then processed peas are back.

Yummy!

2nd April 2020

This could be the new way to meet – same time, same place and you will know it when we start to dress up for the queue. Soon it will feel like normal.

News headlines

Eddie Large's son Ryan has confirmed his ill father's death from COVID-19 after contracting coronavirus in hospital. Eddie, alongside funny man Syd Little, made up one of Britain's most beloved comedy duos, who were known as Little And Large. Their friendship endured for decades, even after they were forced to stop performing together because of Eddie's failing health. He died alone in hospital without his family or friends allowed to visit him due to the strict rules around slowing the spread of the virus.

Love in a queue

I can hardly wait until tomorrow when I'm back here in the queue,
With my trolley ready willing and 2 metres just from you.

I could reach out and touch your shoulder, but I know that would be bad.
Instead of which I blow you kisses. Flip! Just realised, I'm sad.

No more kisses, just loving looks as you queue for things to buy.
And from the way you lean on your trolley, you know I'm here, I sigh.

I got here late the other day and you were already in the queue.
I had to queue behind a stranger. Next time, please wait for me too!!

One day soon you'll turn around, I'll be there, 2 metres still.
Looking for that longing glance, no signs of cough or being ill

And when we leave the till behind, have my rolls, my tablets too.
I don't mind, that's my true love. My sacrifice for you.

Until then I'm off to Boots, another queue and someone new.
I see them too and feel the same, for lovers in the shopping queue.

Move along!

3rd April 2020

There is a feeling that this is going to take off and get bigger as more and more people join in with the clapping. Let's see how it goes.

News headlines

Broadcasters will pause their programming tonight to Clap for our Carers giving the nation a chance to pay tribute to the enduring efforts of the NHS and other key workers across the country once again. The broadcasters will urge members of the public to stand on their doorsteps and balconies and applaud our key workers.

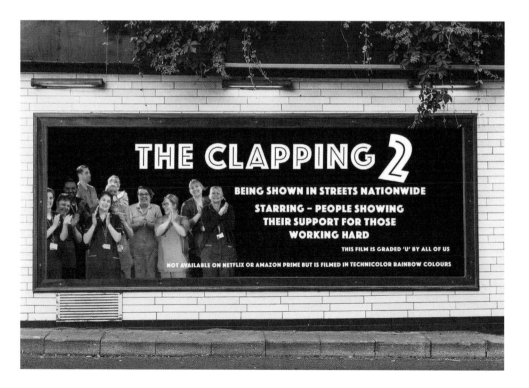

The Clapping Two

Do I feel smug or what? Now my hands are done.
I've clapped with the nation and made up for missing one.

But something is bothering me, I still heard no one else.
Was I now the only one? A lonely clapping self.

Oh no! I've now realised, my mistake again.
I haven't put my clock forward. I'm an hour out, the pain!

I wanted to be part of something and all I am is late.
I can't go back in time you see, standing at my gate.

Last time I wanted help on this, to remind me when to clap.
And I did it right, my 8 o'clock, my individual rap.

So now I promise everyone I'm back in sync with you.
Next week I'll give it everything and the right time, woo hoo!

Until then I'll carry on just ticking off the time.
Maybe I could do a longer one for an hour until nine.

Sorry again

4th April 2020

We are all getting a sense of our new personal space and how important that has become. I sense that is here to stay for a while.

News headlines

British mobile network providers have been forced to debunk 'baseless' theories circulating online that 5G masts are linked to coronavirus after several were set on fire. MobileUK, the trade organisation representing Three, O2, EE and Vodafone, added it was concerned that the pandemic was being used to further such untruths and said some of the industry's key workers are being abused over the unfounded 5G myths. It comes after videos emerged online of phone masts ablaze.

Personal Space

I wonder if you could help me to get my personal space
Not from any people that is; from the human race.

I'm trying to get my dog, Bruce, to work in the other room.
But he keeps right by my side with me, even when I'm using Zoom.

When I tell him it's not dinner or to sit down over there.
He just sits down and stares at me, as if he didn't care.

Anyone would think he liked me, my faithful spotty hound.
But I think it's more the food he wants; more than he's allowed.

You see I have to ration him, in these pressing times.
I've tried so to explain it, in doggy little rhymes.

'No Bruce, you can't have it! Go back to you bed!
It's 5 more hours to dinner'. 'Stop begging 's what I said.

Maybe he could just turn around to give me time to think.
Maybe look out the window, maybe have a drink.

Actually, what am I saying. I wouldn't change a thing.
Can't imagine life without him, all the love that he can bring.

So, I'm not on my own at all. It's me and Bruce as one.
My spotty Dalmatian crazy dog, with me all day long!

And the night as well of course

5ᵗʰ April 2020

What to do about our ever-growing hair is a challenge especially, when like me, some are living alone. Grow it long or cut it short. You decide.

News headlines

Prime Minister Boris Johnson has been admitted to hospital for tests, 10 days after testing positive for coronavirus, Downing Street has said. He was taken to a London hospital on Sunday evening with "persistent symptoms" including a temperature. It is said to be a "precautionary step" taken on the advice of his doctor. The prime minister remains in charge of the government, but the foreign secretary is expected to chair a coronavirus meeting on Monday morning.

My Hair

I've done a rather silly thing; I've gone and cut my hair.
I didn't think about it, I cut without a care.

I used my little trimmer, the one to do my nose.
Not that it's really good at that, my nose hair grows and grows.

But back to my ever growing locks, my trimmer in my hand.
Did I do a little bit, a test to understand?

Just what was the best tactic, to turn my curling locks.
Into something really slick again; instructions in the box.

Of course, I ignored them, just went for it instead.
I grit my teeth and switched it on and stuck it on my head.

So now I have a problem, a reverse Mohican style.
I cut right through the middle; mmm this might take a while.

Sadly, my trimmer failed me, no more battery.
That was when the power went off; it was so not meant to be.

That is why I'm staying, here inside my flat.
Not because of the virus, but because I look like a tw**!

Sorry about the language, but you should see my head.
Should have let it grow long and grey dreadlocks instead.

No FaceTime for a while.

6th April 2020

I am walking Bruce at the times when there is no one else around and when you get over the dark on the river path, we both enjoy it. Clearly, he can see better than me.

News headlines

The Queen has said the UK "will succeed" in its fight against the pandemic and thanked people for staying at home and praised those "coming together to help others". The Queen went on to say: "This time we join with all nations across the globe in a common endeavour, using the great advances of science and our instinctive compassion to heal. We will succeed - and that success will belong to everyone'.

Night walks

I've made a big decision, to walk my dog at night.
It's being socially responsible; it makes me feel just right.

I walk him by the river, he barks if someone's there.
That way I can turn back quick, so, they don't see my hair!

It's not that I'm ashamed at all, I've got a hat you see.
But it's getting hot outside now, so, it's night time walks for me.

I'm slightly worried about Bruce, I think he's quite perturbed.
He sniffs my head and looks away and barks 'that's so absurd'.

'Why would you do that to yourself? How can I walk with you?
Would you mind if you walk on your own? I'm worried what'll you'll do!'

Because you write these poems, I'm dog that's getting known.
I can't be seen with a fool like you and a haircut just half grown.

So, unless you wear a hat all the time, I'm leaving home today
I'll find myself another one with normal hair I say.

So, my friends that is why, I walk my dog at night.
I'll do anything thing for him; a hat will make it right.

And time......

7th April 2020

Whilst it is fun to write light hearted observational poems, sometimes, just sometimes there is a need to briefly change the tone - partly because of just how it is at the moment. Never fear, there are plenty of more stories to come - of course with my best friend Bruce.

News headlines

The number of coronavirus cases in the UK "could be moving in the right direction", the government's chief scientific adviser has said. Speaking at the daily Downing Street briefing, Sir Patrick Vallance said it was "possible that we're beginning to see... the curve flattening". He added, however, it would be another "week or so" before he could be sure. The foreign secretary, meanwhile, said the PM, who is in intensive care, is in "good spirits" and "stable".

I want

I want Boris to get better, I want things as they were.
I don't like this virus thing now; I wish there was a cure.

I want to stop saying unprecedented, in these unprecedented times.
I want to talk about something else, of love and life sublime.

But 'wants' don't always get answers. 'Wants' are not the way.
We have to do the right thing but of course, we're allowed to pray.

We also have to focus and try and stay at home.
Do everything we can to help, look after those alone.

I'm slightly overwhelmed with this, but it's not all negative.
There are many amazing people, with so much to give.

It's not just clapping or washing hands, it's the community for all.
People are standing together; people are standing tall.

One day we will look back on this, one day we will all hold hands.
But for now, let's do our bit, let's do all we can.

Tomorrow's another poem with Bruce and silly hair.
Today I just 'want' to tell you all, just how much I care.

And we all do, even Bruce.

8th April 2020

Eventually this is going to end and when it does and everything is open again, what will you do. Here's a few suggestions.

News headlines

The prime minister has spent a second night in intensive care with coronavirus. According to the latest update on Tuesday evening, he was "stable" and "in good spirits", but being closely monitored. Downing Street has confirmed that given Boris Johnson's illness, the review into the UK's coronavirus restrictions planned for next Monday will now take place at a later date. The curbs on personal freedom, the economy and more were initially imposed for three weeks.

What will you do?

What's the first thing you will do when isolations done?
When everyone is back at work and you're allowed to have some fun.

I fancy a whippy ice cream, with sprinkles chocolate sauce.
And none of it would be complete without double flakes of course.

But then again, a coffee, a blinking big one too.
Not stuck inside my flat, oh no! but sat outside with you.

Hmm, this is really difficult, there's so many things to pick.
Maybe take some time to think, that'll do the trick.

So then, how about this! A pleasant afternoon,
Strolling round the shops again, no messages of doom.

Not a pack of toilet rolls, no headache pills for me.
I'm going to the hairdresser, sort this mess out please!

Oh, the thought of it is wonderful, I hope it's not too long.
To watch the busker play guitar and sing a friendly song.

But most of all there's something else, I want to hold your hand.
To hug you like I love you, now strike up the big brass band.

What will you do?

9th April 2020

Let's get down to some basics. As I manage my supplies, I've made some tiny imperceptible changes to my daily routine. Saves time and money - can't be all bad - you judge!

News headlines

Lockdown extension? It has been two-and-a-half weeks since restrictions on people's movements were announced. And the government's emergency Cobra committee will discuss whether the lockdown ought to be extended beyond its initial three weeks. Leaders of the devolved nations will join the discussions, although First Minister Mark Drakeford has already confirmed measures will remain in place across Wales. With UK temperatures forecast to reach 25C (77F) in place, the public is being urged to "stay home this bank holiday weekend" in a new advertising campaign.

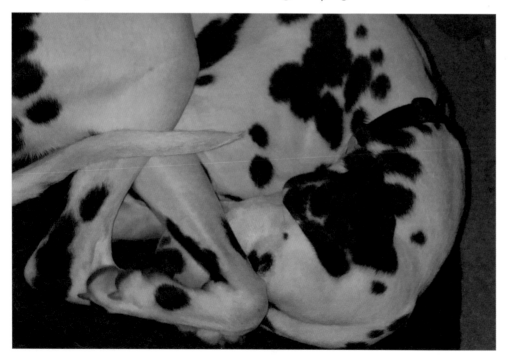

Personal hygiene

I keep the same old clothes on, well what's the point of not.
There's no one here to smell me, except of course, my dog.

It saves on washing powder; it saves on shower gel.
Ok my clothes are 'minging', as far as I can tell.

I'm saving on the water, to keep my meter low.
I've even found another way to make my flowers grow.

I've got loads of aftershave but no one to complement.
So, I say what the heck then, save the environment.

The good thing now is distance, from other people too.
Keeping social spacing, isn't very hard to do.

In fact, they seem to walk away at a rather hasty pace.
Even at the supermarket, it's becoming like a race.

To keep as far as they can, from getting close to me.
But what is sad is not the folks, it's my dog attempt to flee.

Every time I want to stroke him, he wrinkles up his nose,
And goes and sits the other side, as if to say he knows.

Ok! Ok! I'll have a wash but don't go on at me.
I want my tan to be genuine, not stuck on dirt you see.

Sorry about the smell Bruce - Oh well - at least I wash my hands.

10th April 2020

All the days are beginning to merge into one and so holidays of those isolating or staying home are no different from the other day. But it is still Good Friday after all.

News headlines

Prime Minister Boris Johnson has been moved out of intensive care but remains in hospital, Downing Street has said. Mr Johnson has been receiving treatment for coronavirus at St Thomas' Hospital in London since Sunday. No 10 said he "has been moved this evening from intensive care back to the ward, where he will receive close monitoring during the early phase of his recovery". A spokesman added: "He is in extremely good spirits." He was taken to hospital on Sunday - 10 days after testing positive - and was moved to intensive care on Monday.

Bank holiday

Thank heavens it's Good Friday, I can have a long day off,
From my self-isolation. Its sure been long enough.

How do you think I should spend my day? Perhaps I'll stay at home.
That'll make a change then, from being home alone.

In fact, the days all merge now. I've lost my sense of time.
It might just be another day, so, I celebrate offline.

All days are now a holiday, without the queuing cars.
Just queuing for supermarkets, no drinking in the bars.

It's an interesting thought I think, about what day this is.
For Jesus resurrection, three days after this

What would he say if came back now? Need lots of fish and bread,
To send to all the isolators as they lay in their bed.

Actually, I was waiting, for the government to announce.
That Easter had been cancelled, no early springtime dance.

We've moved it to the autumn, or maybe to next year.
The Pope is having a hard time, no crowds to cry or cheer.

Spare a little thought then, plan ahead is what I say.
I'll not get down to DIY, this empty Good Friday.

Instead of which I'll stroke my dog and ring up all my friends.
To wish them happy Easter and hope it soon will end

Happy Easter everyone!

11th April 2020

I live with just Bruce and sometimes sit here and wish I had someone else living with me. However, there are upsides to being alone. Imagine if there were loads together. This is that scenario and I know it's happening.

News headlines

Turkey today began sending planeloads of emergency equipment to Britain to help medics fighting coronavirus. The first flight from Ankara took off today carrying personal protective equipment including surgical masks, N95 industrial masks and hazmat suits, with a second flight due to take off on Saturday, according to the defence ministry. The items were sent in boxes displaying the words of 13th century Sufi Poet Jalaluddin Rumi: 'After hopelessness, there is so much hope and after darkness, there is the much brighter sun.'

The family

Now we're together in our two up two down, we've got to work out what to do.
Our two-seater couch just isn't big enough, now it's more than for just me and you.

Whose idea was it to invite back the kids? They'd all grown up and left home.
The grandparents, Aunt Edna and cousin Keith. It's not quite home alone.

So, we take it turns to sit on the couch, I'm on it tomorrow at three.
Bathroom on Thursday and top tailing in bed, doesn't fill me with lots of glee!

Sunday dinners a joke as we sit on our laps, making it 8 for the chicken roast.
Baked beans we have plenty but doesn't quite go; no potatoes, instead we have toast.

We don't need 'Houseparty', we have it right here. I'm afraid the gin has all gone!
Soon, please soon, can we go out again? But until then what have we done!

I so wish we'd expanded and bought that big house, the one with the ensuite for us.
Then I'd feel better about sharing the soap, praise the lord! No toilet rush!

Until it's all over the family is still here, just can't find Aunt Edna's false teeth.
My darling is ironing and I'm counting loo rolls, and the kids are all playing with Keith.

Families eh - who'd have them - I would!

12th April 2020

Traditional Easter Sunday has been blown away and really brought home to us the huge changes we are coping with at the moment. But if it helps us reflect on what we don't have then when it is back it should be all the sweeter.

News headlines

Lawyers in the US have launched a landmark legal action to sue China for trillions of dollars over the coronavirus pandemic, accusing its Communist leaders of negligence for allowing the outbreak to erupt and then covering it up. The class action, which involves thousands of claimants from 40 countries including Britain and the US, was filed in Florida last month. A second case launched this month on behalf of healthcare workers accuses China of hoarding life-saving medical supplies.

Easter Sunday

No Easter Egg hunts or trips to the park, no visits to the local pub.
No big family dinners or visits today, just all alone Sunday grub.

I'm not at the church apart from online, my singing cannot be heard.
Which is just as well my dog said to me, but my emotions are now really stirred.

You see there are positives, things to be glad, even though I am stuck inside.
It's made me glad that I know you so well and I tell you instead of denied.

This is a time to share our love, for the people that matter to us.
Talk to them, write to them, how do you feel? I feel for you my friend, that's enough.

Lots of people have said it as well, that they've reconnected and love.
I'm not underestimating bad things in the world, but you've given my hand a glove

Have the best Easter you can everyone - I got an Easter egg sent by my boys!!

13th April 2020

I kind of love that all the animals and birds are oblivious to what's going on around them. Bruce things its wonderful because I am home all the time!

News headlines

Comedian, Tim Brooke-Taylor, has died at the age of 79 with coronavirus, his agent has confirmed to the BBC. The entertainer, best known as one third of the popular 1970s show The Goodies, and I'm Sorry I Haven't A Clue, died on Sunday. Goodies co-star Bill Oddie called him a "true visual comic and a great friend".

Birds and bees

Don't get carried away now, this is not about making love.
It's about just what it says, birds and bees and stuff.

About animals and insects, oblivious of the disease.
Have they not seen the briefing, about social distance please?

How come I have to stay apart, if dogs can play around?
If birds can fly in crowded flocks, why can't I hit the town?

You don't see police policing them, with barriers and fines.
They're allowed to make more trips, not stuck in all the time.

I clearly blame the government; I have to blame someone.
They should have clamped down harder, that's what they should have done.

All birds must stay sat in their nests and bees hum in their hives.
They're only allowed 4 times a day, to buzz around and fly.

And don't mention horses, don't get me started there.
Them and cows and pigs as well. They really just don't care.

We're all in this together, that's what they said to us.
But I believe the animals, are driving a different bus.

Don't forget to feed the swans

14th April 2020

I was waiting until the right time to write something about Trump. Quite frankly I could have written it any day. Sleep safe in your bed's, people of the world.

News headlines

On Monday night, Mr Trump gave a combative press conference where he feuded with reporters, criticised their coverage of how he handled the outbreak, and said that when it came to reopen the economy, "the president of the United States calls the shots". "When somebody is the president of the United States, the authority is total," he said, adding: "They can't do anything without the approval of the president of the United States." His position has been contradicted by governors and legal experts.

Donald

'Donald, where's your troosers?' Was a song gone, long ago.
Now the name means something else, a wondrous hairpiece show.

Funny how our leaders are renowned for different hair.
Unless of course you were Churchill without a hairy care.

Anyway, back to Donald and his wavy little hands.
His orange tan and too big suit as he spreads across the land.

I'm rather pleased I'm not from there and an American.
He's in tune with no one, he's an 'I'm the greatest man'.

So, Donald has claimed total power, where did that come from?
Is he some Marvel Avenger? To tweet away what's wrong.

All he wants is four years more to weave his wondrous spell.
Of selling something to the world. What's that? I just can't tell.

Now this is just my musing, of a man that's far away.
I'm sure that if he came to tea, I'd let him have his say.

I'm not doing politics, just sharing thoughts with you.
Tell me to mind to my business and that is what I'll do.

But I'm glad Boris is better now, with our amazing NHS.
You can stick it up your troosers, Donald. With that I say 'god bless'.

EVERYONE in the world - nice wig Bruce!

15th April 2020

However much we sometimes get frustrated by the internet; it is almost impossible to imagine how we could cope at the moment without it. My thanks to technology and www.

News headlines

China has warned it has 'serious concerns' after Donald Trump suspended all US funding to the World Health Organization for what he called 'its role in severely mismanaging the spread of coronavirus'. Beijing's foreign ministry, said the global battle against the pandemic is at a 'critical moment' and that suspending funding will 'undermine international cooperation against the epidemic.' His warning came after President Trump said the US will withhold some $500million in WHO funding while an investigation into its handling of the pandemic is carried out. Trump singled out what he called the WHO's 'dangerous and costly decision' to argue against international travel bans to combat the pandemic.

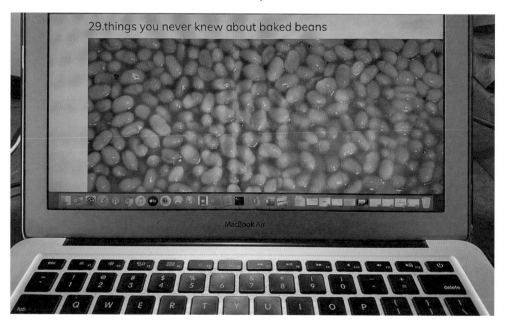

The internet

Let's all bless the internet and all who sail in her
So, the first question that I have, is it a boy or a girl?

Let's assume the webs a girl, don't get lost in that.
More important it's flipping great; I can browse from where I'm sat.

In these times of 'stuck indoors', I have her by my side.
She talks to me, Alexa does, in fact, I must confide...

I offered her my hand today, she turned me down right there.
'I'm not the marrying kind' she said, but I'm not one to despair.

I've connected now with all my friends and made a whole bunch more.
All virtual like, no touching hands, we wave a lot for sure.

I order things that never come, I play games online.
Of course, it's never rude stuff, but it happens all the time!

Not to me though!

But most of it's amazing, to help us all right now.
We've changed so much about ourselves, to the internet I bow.

Was it Mr Berners Lee? Or Tim, if he's your friend.
Whoever it was I thank you now, online friendship till the end.

Flipping screens frozen again Bruce!

16th April 2020

Just once, it would be lovely if Bruce woke up and brought me a cup of tea. Only way is to use my time wisely and introduce a training plan.

News headlines

The UK coronavirus lockdown has been extended by at least three weeks; the Foreign Secretary has confirmed. The senior minister, who is deputising for Prime Minister Boris Johnson as he recovers from Covid-19, said the decision was made following advice from the Scientific Advisory Group for Emergencies (SAGE). The Foreign Secretary said: 'Our action plan aims to slow the spread of coronavirus so fewer people need hospital treatment at any one time and that's the way we can protect the NHS from becoming overwhelmed'.

Dog training

Now I've got lots and lots of time, I'm training Bruce as well.
He can spend it well on clever tasks, like answering the doorbell.

Unfortunately, I've got no bell, but barking works for me.
If people come, but they don't, I know he'll bark for free.

Roll over now, roll back again, go and fetch the ball.
Actually, he's rubbish at that, he leaves it where it falls

So, then I had a cunning plan, to help me start my day.
I'd teach him to make a cup of tea, before we have a play.

No breakfast until I've got from him, a steaming cup of tea.
As you can guess I soon gave up, wasted exercise for me.

So, let's reflect on where I've got, in my doggy training plan.
As long as I do just what he wants, I'm a successful training man.

Equipped to make my dog behave, certificate in the mail.
In the fact the only thing I can do, is make him wag his tail.

That is if I say 'good boy'!

17th April 2020

Remarkable and inspiring at a time when it's what we need. It is also his unassuming nature and all round niceness that seems to resonate with the British public. This is my tribute to Tom.

News headlines

The World War Two hero hit the headlines this week when he set out on raising £1,000 for the NHS by completing 100 laps of his garden before his 100th birthday on 30 April. He began his walks on Monday 6 April and completed his final lap on 16 April. He has smashed his target, raising more than £12.8 million so far. A petition has been set up to see Captain Tom awarded the prestigious title of knight. The petition has already received more than 1,000 signatures from people calling for the 99-year-old to be recognised for his bravery and kindness.

Captain Tom

Captain Tom is an inspiration, quite an incredible man.
Sometimes someone comes along, with a really simple plan.

What's marvellous about our Tom, and he belongs to the nation now.
Is that all he was doing was some exercise, but what a result! Oh wow!

He wanted to raise a little cash, to say thanks for his brand-new hip.
And now with power of viral thingies, he could buy a brand new ship.

So, as he walks around his house, with medals swinging proud.
Total going through the roof, from a funding public crowd.

I've had a chat with my dog Bruce, to see if we could do the same.
Walking on the roof of Superdrug, but that is not the game

We sit instead in awe of Tom, and almost forget his age.
100 years old in a few days more, and still he walks the stage.

Give that man a knighthood, give him a round of applause.
But most of give him a tea, for his quite amazing cause.

We salute you Tom, you British man, you make us proud to smile.
In a time when things are tough for all, you've walked the extra mile!

A salute from Bruce and me! Well a paw from him!

18th April 2020

Our lives' have always been full up, running around, getting stressed. Now, at the moment, we have lots more time. That's when I realised, I have started looking at my clock.

News headlines

At least 15,000 people a day are still travelling to the UK without being checked for coronavirus, the health secretary admitted yesterday. Matt Hancock said the equivalent of 105,000 passengers a week were flying in from countries including China, Italy and the US - all of which have serious outbreaks of the virus. The British government has not imposed any health checks or compulsory quarantine periods in for people arriving into UK airports.

The clock

It's funny I've hardly noticed, the clock upon the wall.
I'm usually rushing around too much, no time to look at all.

But now things are different, and time is on my side.
I spend more time just pausing, to look at life inside.

I've more time to do things, more time to talk to you.
More time to enjoy my box sets, more time sat on the loo.

I can hear my clock ticking, every minute every hour.
Where did all this time come from? So, what will I do now?

I might even have a wash and shave, now I've got the time.
Well not to overdo it, I'm sure I smell just fine.

Now that I'm not rushing, everything I do is slow.
I'm even watching my hair now and hoping it will grow.

And so, the clock is my friend, I'm using up some time.
To write you a daily poem, I hope you like the lines.

So where is your time going? Because we all have more.
Please take time to talk as well, see the clock that's on your wall.

Just a minute Bruce!

19th April 2020

Bruce spends a lot of time looking out of the window and often barks, not just at other dogs, but random passers-by. I wondered why he was barking but now all is clear.

News headlines

Brits will remain in lockdown for another three weeks to slow the spread of the deadly bug - with the UK government reportedly two weeks away from announcing how the country will emerge from the drastic measures But a government source claimed that one plan is to lift the lockdown in phases. Under the possible plans, outdoor spaces would be opened first while pubs would be last. The "best case scenario" could see restrictions eased for non-essential shops from early to mid-May.

Bruce the police dog

Well knock me down with a feather! Bruce is doing his bit.
He's applied to be a police dog not sure what I think of it.

But he was surely adamant that the time had come to act.
So, he's sent his application off, let's see what comes of that.

He wants to be a key dog, an essential canine friend.
By checking on the folk that break, the rules that they will bend.

We know we've got to stay indoors, can't roam the streets at will.
So, Bruce sits by the window, to watch the street until,

If he's sees someone breaking the social distance plan.
He barks at them to step aside, doing all he can.

Now he can only see so far and can't see right below.
So, if you want to confuse him, make sure you only go,

The same side as Superdrug, the shop beneath our home.
That way Bruce will miss you, no reporting on the phone.

He can see right up the High Street, this clever spotty dog.
He makes his notes with diligence on his made-up police dog log.

I'm not sure that he'll get the job, he has a major flaw.
He wags his tail at everyone, not a fearsome dog at all.

The good thing at the moment is that he's so occupied.
Not at all distracted, not a stuck in dog inside.

So, Mr Plod please consider, if you could give Bruce a job,
A special canine constable. Make a proud and spotty dog.

Evening all!

20th April 2020

Now they've started filling all the normal live sports slots with repeats. I guess there are those that miss and those that don't. But it will always be there!

News headlines

Britain's coronavirus lockdown could remain partly in place for a total of three months, the Culture Secretary suggested earlier. Oliver Dowden said this morning that Boris Johnson had stressed back in March he expected the country to be able to "turn the tide" in 12 weeks - and that appears to be what is happening. And he added that the PM was worried about lifting the lockdown restrictions too early and was cautious about changing them. "The PM is very concerned about a second peak if we lift the restrictions too soon".

Sporting repeats

It's seems strange right now to have no sport, that we used to watch on tv.
Not knowing who wins, not knowing the score, instead we get repeats.

Not that I mind and neither does Bruce, but the Olympics would have been good to see.
Meanwhile it's the semi-final match, between Huddersfield and Burnley.

A classic goalless draw it was from 1984.
If only I hadn't seen it, all those years before.

It's the same with all the other sports, classics from years gone by.
So, to keep myself amused, I watch Bruce outstare a fly.

It's a new game I've invented, which is gripping me today.
Sadly, it's not even close now, however hard he plays.

So far, the score is four – nil, to the fly of course, not Bruce.
Not that he's giving up, Oh no! For him there's not a truce,

But I fear that soon it will be over, with the fly just flying away.
Leaving Bruce deflated, looking for a new game to play.

One day the sport will all be back, with rivalries resumed.
Meanwhile I'll carry on watching repeats and the coronavirus news.

Come on Bruce - you can do it!

21ˢᵗ April 2020

There are so many people we are indebted to as they support everyone, despite the risks involved. This is just a small tribute.

News headlines

Sir Richard Branson today warned Virgin Atlantic will need financial aid from the Government in order to survive the coronavirus crisis as he defended himself amid backlash over a bailout request.

Just doing my job

The nurses, the doctors, the porters, the cooks, the carers who look after my aunt.
The cleaners, the people who open the doors, the ones who hold hands when we can't.

The shopkeepers, the postmen and the post ladies too, the dustmen and Captain Tom.
The emergency services who do us so proud, the ones who will work all night long.

The physios, the bakers, the delivery guys, the neighbours who knock on your door.
The friends, the face timers, the unasked for gifts, exercisers wiped out on the floor.

The people who are clever and inventing a cure, the volunteers who pick up the things.
For the people, the elderly and vulnerable too, for the ones who lift spirits and sing

The clappers, the bikers with medicine bags, the presenters, the families as well
The sponsors, the vicars, the makers of masks and the ones who toll the bell

For the ones we have lost

So, we know it's all over and we can go outside. I can step out and walk with my dog
But until then we say thank you to all of you now, who tell us 'I'm just doing my job'

You are amazing!

22nd April 2020

Not difficult to forget, after all her majesty does have 2 birthdays – don't think she will mind.

News headlines

Social distancing measures could remain in place until the end of the year without a vaccine for coronavirus, England's chief medical officer has said. Professor Chris Whitty told the daily Downing Street press conference that some restrictions would need to remain as the probability of having a vaccine or effective drugs to treat the virus within the next calendar year was "incredibly small".

Happy birthday yesterday

Happy Birthday your majesty, official one or not.
I hope you had a lovely day. Sorry I forgot.

I had it on my calendar, but I was distracted by my dog.
He kind of missed the importance, a royal canine fog.

I'm glad you got a birthday card, from Captain Tom, the man.
And Charles, Camilla and the rest of them; the Windsor family clan.

I won't ask about Harry, a touchy subject for sure.
It's the last thing that you needed, now you are 94.

I had a card I promise, I gave it to Bruce to sign.
Sadly, he just ate it, so, the post I must decline.

Never mind it's not important, you've got lots of things to do.
Did you get lots of presents? And lots of cakes for you.

What did Philip get you? Did he make a cup of tea?
Breakfast in beds not what I meant, not my place you see.

Please take good care and isolate, and please look after Phil.
Bruce sends his regards and fondest love, and love to the corgis as well.

Stand up Bruce! National Anthem time.

23rd April 2020

If you look back through music and film history, it is almost as if someone knew what was going to happen.

News headlines

Wales football superstar Gareth Bale has made a remarkable £500,000 donation to help NHS staff in Wales. The Real Madrid forward's gesture was revealed on Wednesday evening as he posted a video online thanking health workers in the country for what they are doing amid the ongoing coronavirus crisis. Bale and his wife Emma have given the huge sum of money to the official NHS charity of Cardiff and Vale Health Board. The charity focuses on providing extra services for patients and staff that normal NHS funds don't provide.

Times, they are a changin'

I don't suppose Bob Dylan, when he wrote those famous words,
Realised that it works today, in our mixed up crazy world.

My dog is unaware of all, he knows only love and food.
I wish in a way I was like him too, not a fragile human fool.

We have no idea how tomorrow, will look or feel for us.
What we know is for sure, we have plenty to discuss.

Discuss about our journey, we have shared along the way.
Discuss about our taxes, how much we'll have to pay.

I just want to come out the other side, to greet you with a hug.
Think that might be quite a while, coffee shops and coffee mugs.

I believe the most important thing, is not to forget this time.
It may seem really obvious, but I worry down the line

Wars have come and wars have gone, we forget that lives are lost.
The human race could forget this day, this coronavirus host.

But tomorrow will come I'm sure it will, so let's prepare for that.
And after all the street parties, remember where you're sat.

Sat in isolation, but reached out as friends.
I want to carry on with that, carry on until the end.

Can't imagine having a tail though!

24th April 2020

As someone who is self isolating I am extremely grateful for those that have helped me to deliver food. Trouble is I'm tired of bread, eggs and milk.

News headlines

President Trump proposed unorthodox new treatments for the virus at Thursday's White House press briefing – including injecting cleaning agents in the body and use of ultraviolet lights. Trump asked a senior Homeland Security science and technology advisor: 'Supposing we hit the body with a tremendous, whether it's ultraviolet or just very powerful light? And I think you said, that hasn't been checked but you're going to test it. And then I said supposing you brought the light inside the body which you can do either through the skin or in some other way. And I think you said you're going to test that too. Sounds interesting.'

The shopping list

Thank you for doing my shopping, as I personally isolate.
I've made a list of essential things, that I need on my plate.

I've kept it very simple, just basic things I need.
So, let me give them to you, as you and I agreed.

I'm still ok on baked bean tins, I've still got mushy peas.
So let's start with what's critical, 'running out' of if you please.

Obviously, I need some salt, the Himalayan mountain one.
Organic truffles, Logan jam, frosted brioche buns.

I've nearly run out of vanilla pods, running low on Serrano ham.
And I would like some guavas please, grateful if you can.

Oh, I forgot the pickled ginger, ground spicy Tuscan beans.
Of course, I need some toilet roll, scented lavender dreams.

Bruce would like most anything, if it's shaped just like a bone.
But then again, he shares with me, though he leaves the beans alone.

I think I've done the basics, anymore I'll let you know.
Oh, there is just one more tiny thing, a chocolate bar to go.

Big one please and not dog chocolate!

25ᵗʰ April 2020

Some mornings I wake up and have to pinch myself that this is real and not something else instead. If you were telling someone about a dream you had, or maybe a nightmare, would they believe you.

News headlines

Kim Jing-Un, North Korea's Supreme Leader is dead - according to multiple sources coming out of North Korea and the Far East, though due to the hyper-secretive nature of the pariah state the exact picture remains unclear tonight. It was being reported as fact by media outlets in China and Japan that the 36-year-old dictator was dead. Sources said he was on his death bed in a vegetative state with no hope of resuscitation after botched heart surgery. Because of the nature of the ultra secret regime in North Korea claims of Kim Jong-un s death are very difficult to verify.

The dream

You'll never guess but I woke up today and realised it was all a dream.
I'd dreamt we'd all been stuck indoors and couldn't go out; it seems.

I know it's hard to believe for sure, but you know what dreams are like.
They seem bizarre and bonkers. Just call me crazy Mike!

In my dreams there'd been this thing, a global pandemic.
It was like the film 'Contagion', where everyone was sick.

Only, there were no stars in this dream but get this, this bit's strange,
Our PM, Boris Johnson was sick and quite deranged.

Ok, that's not so hard to believe, but there's more I tell you now.
I'd started walking my dog at night and only ate beans for chow.

I'd cut bits off my greying hair and looked a bit of a fool.
I'd clapped at no one for many hours and all the kids left school.

No one was working but parks were full, and cinemas were shut.
You couldn't drink latte outside anymore, I know you think I'm nuts.

Fortunately, I woke up, from this dream I had.
The sun is out, I'll watch the news and then get on, I'm glad.

Oh shucks, it wasn't a dream!

26th April 2020

At first it doesn't seem to matter and then when you realise that it has been over 4 weeks since any human contact, you crave it more. It's the same for anything that you can't have and I don't just mean fast food!

News headlines

Home secretary Priti Patel's announcement that the level of shoplifting has fallen compared to the year before has baffled viewers of the latest government press briefing. In her second appearance in front of cameras at Downing Street since the coronavirus outbreak hit, the home secretary said there had been a fall in overall crime during the outbreak, with "car crime, burglary, shoplifting" lower than the same period last year.

Touch

I so just want to touch you, feel skin on skin again.
It's not rude to want it. It might help me feel sane.

A hand held means so much now, because it's not allowed.
At first it didn't matter, but I was wrong somehow.

And oh! To hug you close once more, feel your breath upon my face.
All so wrong but miss it so, fundamental for our race.

I haven't touched you for a month, but it's still not normal yet.
The longing never goes away, despite what experts said.

I'd cover myself in sanitiser, if it meant I could touch you.
Ok the smell might linger, but you could do it too.

Let me ask the scientists if it's ok to try,
I know, I know the answer. Do it and you'll die!

Not from touching necessarily, but from too much cleaning gel.
Like trump advised injections, to disinfect as well.

So, until it's allowed again, I'll wave and make heart signs.
I love you still and always will, in these non-touching times.

Fortunately, I can stroke my dog.

27th April 2020

The very idea that someone would deliberately get themselves sent to jail to allow a degree of protection is so absurd that just maybe....

News headlines

The UK is at the moment of maximum risk in the coronavirus outbreak, Boris Johnson has said, as he urged people not to lose patience with the lockdown. Speaking outside No 10 for the first time since recovering from the virus, Mr Johnson said "we are now beginning to turn the tide" on the disease. But he said he refused to "throw away" the public's "effort and sacrifice" and relax the lockdown too soon.

Self isolating prisoner

He stole a lot of toilet roll, that was his only crime.
He did it for a reason. He was happy to do some time.

He reckoned that he could isolate and be safe from nasty germs.
Have a cosy cell all to himself, but he made a mistake, he learned.

He shared a cell with another, a forger from Bethnal Green.
Together they made an alliance, to self-isolate as a team.

The prison psychologist checked him out, to see what was in his mind.
It wasn't complicated, he loved the rolls, and the feeling on his behind.

Now he wasn't expecting the life he had to be perfect and lots of fun,
But the hours just didn't suit him. He wanted to go on the run.

So, the forger made him some documents, to get him out of jail.
He pretended to be a key worker, deliver parcels for the mail

Soon he was on the outside, back on civvy street.
You'd think he'd have learnt his lesson, about who he shouldn't meet.

Sadly, he couldn't help it. The lure of toilet rolls,
Was too much for our dodgy fella, and the prison bells still tolls.

So now he's back inside again. This time it's a single cell.
And so, he got his self-isolation, so, for him it turned out well.

But don't go getting ideas, about doing illegal things.
In the end you'll end up isolated. That's what stealing brings.

And there's lots of loo rolls now.

28th April 2020

The other day I watched Jesus Christ Superstar on YouTube and it was quite spectacular - looking forward to more – so it made sense to write a poem about another famous musical and somehow it connected to where we all were and are now.

News headlines

A minute's silence will be held across the UK later to commemorate the key workers who have died with coronavirus. Boris Johnson, who returned to work on Monday, will join the tribute, which starts at 11:00. More than 100 NHS and care staff have died with the virus. It comes as the son of a doctor who died called on the government to issue a public apology for issues with personal protective equipment.

Empty chairs at empty tables (Les Mis)

Don't think I'm going to sing to you or be miserable instead.
I'm just reflecting what is not, of the lives that we have led.

We can think what we don't have and eating out is one.
Of coffee cups and muffin breaks, of chatting in the sun.

But we don't have commuter crowds. Bet you don't miss that time.
But cheering crowds at football grounds, the ball has crossed the line,

And changed our lives forever. I hope for good I pray.
We look at things in different ways and not just for today.

And so, whilst there are many things, too many to list them all.
Of things we've lost or put on hold, that is not the call

Be glad for things you still can do, virtual theatre on YouTube.
People who have reconnected, and many friendships new.

I look forward to the time, when I can meet you on a walk.
Just me and Bruce and everyone, be close enough to talk.

The restaurant days will be back soon. Chairs and tables full.
I'll have a plate of what you've got. Let's not be miserable.

Tried to do a poem on 'Cats' but Bruce growled.

29th April 2020

In just a short time those sunny days we had in most of April disappeared, but they will be back. For some it doesn't matter anyway with Lockdown! So, this is through the eyes of one such person. Today your casual poet brings you another British obsession.

News headlines

Prime Minister Boris Johnson and his fiancée Carrie Symonds have announced the birth of a son. A spokeswoman for the PM and his partner said both mother and baby are "doing very well". It is understood the PM, who has just recovered from coronavirus, was present throughout the birth, at an NHS hospital in London. The couple have received messages of congratulation from across the political spectrum, and the PM's father Stanley said he was" absolutely delighted" and "thrilled" by the birth of his grandson.

And here is the weather...

I like the weather now I'm in my flat, it hasn't rained at all.
Cold fronts have gone and whistling wind, no weather warnings at all.

Ok we've just had our summer, like the time I went to Spain.
But now it's not so bright outside and I'm indoors again.

My picnic plans are set in stone, as long as I stay inside.
Sticky buns and cups of tea to drink, no wasps to wave aside.

Haven't had fog for days now. A little bit of red mist though.
That was more to do with me and stubbing my big toe!

On the picnic table, I dragged inside my flat.
Maybe that was too much but done now so that's that.

I had a heatwave last night. No, not the fever one.
I messed up the thermostat timing, like an oven roasted bun.

So, 'here is the weather' doesn't interest me, apart from thunderstorm signs.
They mess my internet reception; my box sets on amazon prime.

I predict a long hot summer, whenever that will be.
Plan to be outside then, my picnic table and me.

Glass of lemonade Bruce?

30th April 2020

There is only one thing your casual poet could possibly write today and for the second time! The nation is excited to go to his party and share the 100 candles - so here we go Captain, no Colonel Tom.

News headlines

Captain Tom Moore, the war veteran who raised millions for the NHS by walking laps of his garden, has been made an honorary colonel on his 100th birthday. The occasion has also been marked with an RAF flypast and birthday greetings from the Queen and prime minister. Captain Tom was also informed of his promotion to honorary colonel in a letter presented by Lt Col Thomas Miller, commanding officer of the 1st Battalion, The Yorkshire Regiment, at his home. Captain Tom said it was "extraordinary" to be turning 100, especially with "this many well-wishers". With celebrations under way, the total he has raised for NHS Charities Together topped £30m.

Not missing your birthday

I know I missed her majesty's, but I wasn't going to miss this one
So happy birthday, Mr important man. Happy birthday, Captain Tom!

One of things I like about you, is that you don't like to make a fuss.
I get the feeling you're always like that, but we've still got lots to discuss.

So, you walked the line around your house and did it a hundred times.
But that pales into nowt my friend for what you put on the line.

When you served as you did in India, during all of World War 2.
For the Yorkshire regiment and all of them, and for other things you would do!

You raced motorbikes; you organised your regiment reunion for years
64 to be precise but numbers are naught, compared to your good cheer

You've now had a number one song you have. The oldest man ever for that.
The fact you took it off Tom Jones as well, to the 2 Toms I raise my hat!

But for 'Just Giving' dear Tom you've blown it all, every record from long away
I won't even record the millions you've raised 'cos' it keeps going up every day

You may get a knighthood or an OBE, but I know that it's no matter to you
For you, Colonel Tom, are already the man, so happy birthday from everyone too!

Have you seen just how many birthday cards you've got! And a train!

1st May 2020

Just imagine if this virus had happened at Christmas or, horror of horrors, the lockdown had been that long. So instead of 1st May we were celebrating a different day.

News headlines

The government is likely to meet or "come close" to its target of 100,000 daily coronavirus tests, Communities Secretary Robert Jenrick has said. Health Secretary Matt Hancock said the government would achieve the aim by the end of April - which was Thursday - and those figures are expected later. Just over 81,000 tests took place on Wednesday, but ministers said there was capacity for more.

Festive greetings

It'll soon be Christmas and another year almost done.
Just imagine if it really was, instead it's May begun.

I can't imagine a Christmas party, no jingle bells or festive now.
I know we'd make the best of it and decorate somehow.

Only plastic Christmas trees dragged down from dusty lofts.
Lights with no replacement bulbs, decorate with what you've got.

Christmas elves and Santa, as key workers themselves,
Might start delivering with Amazon to help maintain his health.

Let's face he must isolate, given his age and life.
Travelling is much harder with border closure rife.

Lots of virtual presents, to cut down on the cost.
Carol concerts sang online, individual bits of frost.

Some people say it's like it now, between Christmas and New Year.
Quiet streets and naff TV and isolating cheer.

I'm sure we'll long have moved on, before our Christmas Eve.
So, we can celebrate baby Jesus, or whatever we believe.

As long as we remember those stuck on their own.
Please send me some more mince pies, to my jolly festive home.

Merry Christmas Bruce

2nd May 2020

For many of us, cars have become less important and, even if it's just been for a while, I've enjoyed not seeing long queues. Wonder how long that will be. Not long I bet.

News headlines

More than 6,500 people have registered their interest to take part in a UK trial to see if blood plasma from coronavirus survivors can treat hospital patients with Covid-19. The hope from the trial, which has now started, is that the antibodies recovered patients have built up will help clear the virus in others. Last week, NHS Blood and Transplant began collecting blood from survivors.

Start your engines

Well I'm not putting miles on my car right now, just dirt and dropping birds.
I'm a safer driver too which is good, empty roads if you haven't heard.

Not that it's stopped the odd one or two, on roads and country tracks.
They drive like racing drivers, to the supermarket and back.

But my car sits and waits for me, easing the battery away.
And when the time comes to start her up there's not a chance she'll play.

So, then I will ask for a hand my friend, to help push start my car.
And just in case you are worried, I'll watch you from afar.

Ok that doesn't work so let's try this, I can sit inside whilst you strain.
I wish I hadn't eaten all the biscuits; you might have to push again.

And then when the engines started, I'm off to get some grub,
Whilst you are panting and sweating, you can guess what's coming up.

The ambulance will take you away, to check that you are well.
Then you'll have to isolate again, while I'm on the 'road to hell'

Thanks, Chris Rea, for that one.

3rd May 2020

The wonder of technology provides us with amazing opportunities to connect. But...its not real and boy do I want that. I told a friend that I would hug the first person I saw as soon as we can - might get into trouble!

News headlines

A man has been arrested after protesters in London took part in a group hug outside Met Police's headquarters in defiance of the coronavirus lockdown. The crowd outside New Scotland Yard were seen hugging each other as others held signs reading: "My body, my choice." and "No more lockdown." Police told the protesters to go home before arresting a man who did not comply. Gatherings of any sort are banned under the UK's rules to slow the spread of coronavirus which were rolled out on March 23.

Virtual

I'm sick of flipping virtual with most things that I do.
I want the real thing now please and no more virtual you.

I want you right here by my side, not some emoji smiling face.
And virtual hugs are limited, they can hardly fill the space.

I know that technological and longer words than that,
Provide me with lots of things except for where I'm sat.

I guess I am still grateful for virtual reality.
But my real worlds slightly empty, without you next to me.

I'd like one virtual thing please that was virtual to the top.
And that's my bulging biscuit tin. Stop eating Mike, please stop!

And Bruce he isn't virtual, so all things aren't so bad.
I've got a real dog by my side; he stops me getting sad.

There is just one small thing, that I wish he didn't do.
And look away now if you want, but I'd prefer virtual poo.

And so, I send my virtual thoughts as we plod along.
Keep going for a little while more back where we once belong.

Sending you some virtual emoji love from Bruce and me.

4th May 2020

Many of us are pondering where we might want to go on holiday after the Lockdown. Not entirely sure myself. And at the moment it feels like a really long holiday at home.

News headlines

Reduced hot-desking and alternatives to social distancing where it is not possible are among measures being considered to let workplaces reopen. A draft government plan to ease anti-coronavirus restrictions, seen by the BBC, also urges employers to minimise numbers using equipment, stagger shift times and maximise home-working. PM Boris Johnson is to reveal a "roadmap" out of lockdown on Sunday.

Summer holiday booked

I don't know about you, but I know what I want and that's a holiday when this is all done.
Trouble is, my plan's up the spout, the Italian villa in the sun.

The trip to the Seychelles isn't on now, nor the road trip on Route 66.
In fact, I surmise, I have to rethink, about all my options for trips.

Who knows how many aeroplanes there will be, and which country will let me in?
Should I take a cruise Nah! Not for me! And no strolling around Beijing.

Group holidays are no more with tour guides gone; city breaks are a thing of the past.
Ok I know they will come back one day, maybe I shouldn't have asked.

I do however have a cunning plan, and yes, you've guessed it I'm sure.
It is me and my dog walking somewhere, a lovely self-isolating tour.

We will go somewhere where there's no one else, just not sure where that is
Perhaps it's a beach, perhaps it's a hill, perhaps it's just where I live.

Whatever happens, wherever I am, I have booked it in my mind.
That's because all the tourist agencies are closed, I think you'll find.

Some of time it feels like it just now, like an extended holiday at home.
So, I can sit outside and close my eyes and let my imagination roam.

Pack your bags Bruce - we're staying here

5th May 2020

When I've watched people in the street; contact is now very different from before the outbreak and even more so in the supermarkets – I know it will get better and it is already, but for now this is my observation.

News headlines

An NHS app that aims to track the spread of coronavirus is being rolled out for the first time, as part of a trial on the Isle of Wight. Council and healthcare workers will be the first to try the contact-tracing app, with the rest of the island able to download it from Thursday. If successful, it could be available nationwide within weeks. Concerns have been raised over privacy, though ministers say the app has been designed with this "front of mind". The app aims to quickly trace recent contacts of anyone who tests positive for the virus.

Don't look at me

Now I walk the streets alone, with distance as my friend.
People don't look up anymore, no friendly glance to send.

We avoid any eye contact at all, small gestures are all I get.
It's as if we've vanished, as if we'd never met.

Does it make us feel better, trapped in our little world?
If I don't look, I won't get sick, my sanity unfurled.

It's like a double conflict, I'm lonely in my home.
But when I walk in shopping aisles, I keep myself alone.

And yet I want to see you and feel your smile on me.
I miss the human contact; I miss what we could be.

I understand the caution, to not breathe near your face.
But let me smile into your eyes, as we walk by at pace.

Maybe a little gesture, a thumb raised to the sky.
I see you and I care for you, as we are passers-by.

One day we will shake hands again, and speak 'how have you been?'
But for now, let's glance and nod and then you'll know I've seen,

You...look at me Bruce!

6th May 2020

There has been real shortage of alcohol in the supermarkets – wonder why!
And we rushed to buy toilet rolls! This online entertainment is our salvation.

News headlines

*Former Prime Minister Theresa May has criticised world leaders for failing
"to forge a coherent international response" to the coronavirus pandemic.
"Lack of international collaboration could lead to the world becoming more
dangerous" she warned. A No 10 source said there had been "extensive
co-operation", with the PM talking regularly to other G7 leaders. Mrs May's
intervention comes as Boris Johnson and Sir Keir Starmer face each other at
Prime Minister's Questions for the first time later.*

Online glass of wine

I couldn't wait to meet you and drink pints at the pub.
Well we can't of course do that, no more country grub.

No basket meals or peanuts, sat in crowded bars
Instead of which we drink online, with FaceTime from afar.

The blessing of this distant drink is buying drinks for all!
'Whose round is it?' is long gone, no 'last orders' call!

So now we can drink all through the night, smiling down our phones,
And when the image is blurry, blame on calls that roam.

So, you drink white and I'll drink red and I'll eat crisps for two.
I'll dress up in a dinner suit, a cocktail dress for you.

You can have your pickled onions and don't have to hold your nose,
Even though I've eaten garlic bread, my smell you'll never know.

So though were not together, I'm drinking with my friend.
One day we'll do this outside, I'll toast you to the end.

Cheers!

7th May 2020

I know I've written about key workers before with 'Just doing my job' but they continue to amaze me with their dedication. So, for any of you key workers out there, I want to say it again – just with some different words.

News headlines

The PM says the government will proceed with "maximum caution" when considering easing coronavirus restrictions. Boris Johnson is due to announce plans for England's lockdown on Sunday, but ministers have insisted short term changes to measures will be "modest". At the government's daily briefing, Foreign Secretary Dominic Raab described media reports on easing restrictions as "not a reliable guide". He added that changes may vary between the different nations.

Key worker

I know you are a key worker, but I don't know your name.
I'm sorry if I take you for granted, my excuse is rather lame.

It's because you're always there for me, you never let me down.
Whatever you are doing, you never have a frown.

So, when I clap on Thursdays, or at any other time.
When I just say I thank you, for being very kind.

It goes much deeper I guess, you're critical to me.
I don't know what I'd do without you and I'm glad that I can see,

Real goodness in the world today, despite this COVID thing.
Real goodness in you my friend, the wonder that you bring.

This isn't a time to joke around and make some little jest.
Thank you from the bottom of my heart, you really are the best

And that's for all of you!

8th May 2020

I wanted to write a wondrous celebration about 75 years since the end of WWII. Well, we are indomitable as a people so get out the scones and jam and bunting and do it! For now, if not for then.

News headlines

The UK is to mark the 75th anniversary of VE Day, with the Royal Family leading tributes as the country remains in lockdown due to the coronavirus. The Prince of Wales and the Duchess of Cornwall will lead a two-minute silence at 11:00 BST to honour servicemen and women during World War Two, and the Queen will address the nation later. The PM thanked the VE Day generation, saying "our gratitude will be eternal".

VE day 75th anniversary

The sound of the spitfire, the beat of the drum, as we celebrate 75 years.
Since victory in Europe, armistice signed, we should have much to cheer.

But somehow it feels hollow, and not as it should, no street parties like back then.
No toasting drinks or sailors kiss, just strangeness now my friend.

Imagine if you can, what they would say, of how the world is now.
For victory day think virus instead but think positive somehow.

So, let's do it right like only we can, the spirit and grit we know
We can distance ourselves but not be down and put on a great big show

Because we must, we really must, and not dwell on the past.
Of course, we can shake a flag or two, but clapping has to last.

Many know not what was done, all those years ago.
So VE day is meaningless, for the 'lockdown over' show.

Then maybe, many years from now, people will raise a cheer.
For how we coped with COVID time, and what we did right here.

I served my time for many years, in Royal Air Force blue.
But now I want to walk outside and be virus free with you.

On a dog walk of course!

9th May 2020

One of the huge positives about this lockdown period is the number of people who've made time to exercise. When it's over I hope you can keep it up. I'm with you all the way...

News headlines

UK airlines say they have been told the government will bring in a 14-day quarantine for anyone arriving in the UK from any country apart from the Republic of Ireland in response to the coronavirus pandemic. The new restriction is expected to take effect at the end of this month. Industry body Airlines UK said the policy needed "a credible exit plan" and should be reviewed weekly.

Keeping fit

I've worked out an exercise programme, that I think is perfect for me.
It involves a lot of running and of course, a cup of tea.

Firstly, lots of stretching. How you say, 'get down with dog'.
Then I get Bruce to touch my toes, it's really not a slog.

If you have to stay inside and not venture out of doors.
Then run around the kitchen, do press ups on the floor.

Bend those knees, I do that well, as I'm sitting on my couch.
My fingers flexing on my phone. Don't call me a slouch.

You see my exercise programme, is just for Bruce to do.
I make sure that he keeps fit. You didn't think me, did you?

Of course, I'm not completely lazy, I walk around a bit.
Mostly to the fridge and back. Back to the couch to sit.

I make sure Bruce gets rewards, for running round the flat.
He's done a 100 laps now. Will he get a cricket hat?

Like the amazing Captain Tom did, now there's a fit young man.
I'm a bit fatigued now, with my doggy fitness plan

So, I'd better take a rest now, tea and biscuit break.
This exercising far too hard, it's keeping me awake

Come on Bruce - put some effort into it!

10th May 2020

I always knew that at some point I had to acknowledge the real impact of this terrible virus. I, like many of you, I am sure, know someone who has passed on or been affected by COVID-19. As your casual poet, these are my thoughts as we wait until it is over. This is my 2 minute silence.

News headlines

An alert system to rank the threat level of coronavirus in England is set to be launched by Prime Minister in his lockdown speech. The system, which will use a scale of one to five and be adjusted according to data, is to be as part of the PM's televised address. Mr Johnson will also explain any changes to the lockdown measures. It comes after he introduced a new slogan, telling the public to "stay alert, control the virus, save lives".

Numbers

They are not numbers, the women the men, the boys and girls I have known.
They are my friends, my neighbours, my kin, o I say that you're not alone.

This is no time for statistics or graphs. This is the time to draw breath.
We reflect on your life, wherever you were, this is so not about your death.

But let's not pretend this is the happiest of times, I wish you were still with me today.
To share my life as you did before, instead you have gone away.

I promise you this. I will make of my life, use it up with the fullness of you.
You've passed on the mantle to all of us now, there is so much that we have to do.

This is a new world we find ourselves now, as the sun shines down from above.
But I will remember, I promise you this, not a number but someone to love.

We will not forget

11th May 2020

The more I think about it, when I see politicians and people offering advice, good or bad, there is a common theme. And that's not what they say, but what's behind them. I'm sure I'm not the only one.

News headlines

People in England can meet up with others outside their household in the outdoors as long as they stay 2m apart, the government has confirmed. Foreign Secretary Dominic Raab urged people to "use some common sense" and people cannot visit others at home. The new rule is part of a 50-page guidance document to be published by the government later.

The bookcase

I love it when the clever people, talk to us from their homes.
How do I know they're clever, as they're talking on their phones?

Why it's obvious really isn't it, it's the bookcase right behind.
Anyone with a bookcase, must have a clever mind

Do they think we're fooled, about how we think of them?
I'm more interested in their haircuts, and not literary gems.

I did watch Stephen Fry advise, about how to fill your time.
And bizarrely no books behind him, and his advice sublime.

He doesn't need to prove he's clever, we already know.
It's the silly ones that do it, the politician show.

I might get myself a bookcase, just in case I need.
To read a little poem, on daytime tv feed.

Ok, it won't happen, but just in case I will,
Buy some books off eBay. Wouldn't that be brill.

I could always buy some flowers or a potted plant.
Maybe get some plastic ones, with my imaginary business grant.

Meanwhile I'll stick Bruce behind. He distracts from what I say.
Then you'll like me just a bit, as long as he will stay.

Bruce - STAY! Shucks he's gone.

12th May 2020

I listened to someone on the tv mention the noise of the birds in the morning and how our sounds have changed. As they begin to revert back to normal – we can still ask the question.

News headlines

This year's summer solstice celebrations at Stonehenge in southern England have been cancelled because of the ban on mass gatherings prompted by the coronavirus. Traditionally about 10,000 people gather at the Neolithic monument in Wiltshire, on or around 21 June, to mark midsummer. English Heritage said it was cancelling the event "for the safety and wellbeing of attendees, volunteers and staff". The occasion will instead be live streamed on the charity's social media accounts.

Keep the noise down?

Please could everyone help me and drive your cars again.
I need to hear the traffic noise, to help to keep me sane.

Instead my ears are hurting, with other deafening sounds.
It's the birds and what they're doing. Aren't they meant to be shut down?

And I'm tired of babbling brooks as well, and the hum of buzzing bees.
And don't get me started with the wind, and the rustling in the trees.

Bring back the crowds of chanting at football grounds and all.
Children playing with laughter, fairground hammers fall.

We've had the sound of spitfires, to stir our pride and chest.
We've heard the sound of clapping as we applaud the NHS.

So, no more silent moments please, with time for long reflect.
I want the noise of business, normal noises we expect.

Until then I'll listen hard, for different noise again.
And take my dogs for long walks as he barks along the lane.

Shhhh…Bruce isn't that a plane?

13th May 2020

A writer called Aldous Huxley wrote 'A Brave New World' in 1932, his vision of dystopia, which, when I looked it up, is not a great place. Ring any bells?

News headlines

People in England who cannot work from home are being encouraged to return to their workplaces today, as the UK government begins easing some lockdown measures. Under the new rules, garden centres can also reopen, and people can meet one person from outside their household. Meanwhile, people can spend more time outside, meet a friend at the park, and move home. But the changes don't apply in Scotland, Wales and Northern Ireland - where the message remains "stay at home".

Now what Aldous Huxley?

This is not a brave new world, it's the one we left behind.
Everything's still sitting there, ready to unwind.

We've haven't got to invent things, like the wheel and mobile phones.
Washing machines are not new, in our technological homes.

But we have to change so much we do; from the way we were before.
And how and what is up to us, when we step out the door.

I don't know all the answers, only a fool knows that.
And the world was foolish before this time, so where does that leave us at?

They said we would move to normal, but a new one, nevertheless.
How do we know what that is? How do we measure our success?

So, what is new is just that. We set new benchmarks now.
We decide the standard of our life, so let us show them how.

But please, oh please, remember, the longing felt inside.
Inside during lockdown, when emotions were defied.

I will try my best as well, to be the man I used to be
But also, I will aim much higher, I'm a new man can't you see?

Yes, Bruce you're a new dog too.

14th May 2020

I've written about the noise of the birds before but there is a bigger impact to our planet because of what's happened. I wonder how long to will last.

News headlines

An antibody test has been approved by health officials in England. Public Health England said the antibody test was a "very positive development". The blood test looks for antibodies to see if a person has already had the virus and might now have some immunity.

Pollution free

Slightly ironic if that's the term, that we've started to clean up our act.
Less cars, less planes and factories, and the air is cleaner - fact!

Maybe that will appease the greens, but it certainly appeases me.
I love the fact the air quality is good, just worried about virus seed.

It's a reflection on us and the planet, that it has taken something like now.
To take us back to a better time, when life was simpler somehow.

Roads are quieter, the sky is clear, just people enjoying the park.
How do we ensure that it stays for us, that we can hear the sound of the lark?

Somehow, I suspect the queues will reform, congestion and pollution will come back.
Maybe, just maybe, we will learn from this, as we return and get back on track.

But whatever it takes and however long, if we've stopped chopping down the trees,
I'm glad for that time when we stopped the rush, more honey will come from the bees.

Love a bit of honey on my toast.

15th May 2020

It's the new way to communicate, so you can work and chat even when you are at home. Does it work for you? As long as you make sure you are dressed! This is my observation…

News headlines

Teachers' unions are to meet the government's scientific advisers later to seek assurances that it will be safe to open schools in England. The education secretary wants primary schools to begin opening from 1 June. But the National Education Union's Kevin Courtney said parents and teachers needed to be "absolutely clear" about the "level of safety". Meanwhile, one of England's biggest academy trusts says it will go ahead with opening its schools on 1 June.

Zoom

Isn't zoom amazing and what it helps us do.
Talk to lots of people, share moments me and you.

Well perhaps it isn't perfect, or rather I mean us.
I haven't quite mastered no quite on the bus.

In fact, we spend a lot of time, looking at our face.
Checking that we look ok, and not look out of place.

I try and look intelligent; I turn my head a bit.
Sage looks and knowing thoughts I show at my computer as I sit.

Sometimes I don't know what to say, how to join in the call.
I fumble and go quiet, instead of on the ball.

And them sometimes I forget, forget to mute my voice.
And then Bruce barks at postmen, or another bottom noise.

Until then I'll pretend to be, a conference master man.
Enthused and dedicated, smiling all I can.

If it's what we've got today, let's make of it the best.
Switch it on and brush our hair, on this communication test.

Actually, you look great Bruce.

16th May 2020

We seem to have forgotten about Brexit and it all seems a little irrelevant now. I wonder if it will be completed by the end of the year. I have my thoughts about that.

News headlines

Comet Swan and its 11 million mile long tail will be visible in the night sky from tonight and you may be able to see it with the naked eye, astronomers say. The ball of ice, discovered in April, has already passed the Earth but is getting brighter as it approaches the Sun. It will be best viewed from the southern hemisphere, but those in the northern hemisphere will still be able to see it low on the horizon in the pre-dawn hours.

Brexit at last

So, let's talk about Brexit, nothing better to do.
The paint is dry, the sheep asleep, so, I've plenty of time for you.

I'd almost forgotten about it, what does it mean right now?
I haven't just lost the EU, my contacts gone somehow.

I'm not isolated from Europe; I'm isolated from friends.
I've performed my own separation. A mini Brexit at the end.

There was no vote, no exit poll, we did it as it made sense.
But do we need to ratify, this kind of life suspense.

There are few things good about this virus, this once in a lifetime thing.
But that's what they said about Brexit, and the things that it might bring.

Separation was the main thing, and a chance to start again.
Restriction on people's movements, Border controls to contain.

Well knock me down with a feather, it's seems we've done it so.
Brexit and virus together, a double whammy show!

That was a party-political broadcast on behalf of me and my dog.

17th May 2020

The tragedy of the virus in our care homes has been enormous. It breaks my heart to think about the families, the carers and the elderly who we thought were safe in their last days.

News headlines

Former US President Barack Obama has criticised his successor Donald Trump's handling of the coronavirus crisis. In an online address to graduating college students, he said the pandemic had shown that many officials "aren't even pretending to be in charge". It is the second time in recent days that Mr Obama has hit out at the Trump administration's coronavirus response. He said it had been "an absolute chaotic disaster" during a leaked conference call last week.

I care

I care about the care homes, and what they have become.
That's because of Aunty Edna, but what I fear we've done.

I wish, I wish, she'd not gone there, and wish she was with me.
I now can't see her like I did, it wasn't meant to be.

It was somewhere that she would feel safe, safe with all her friends.
And now her friends aren't there now, with the Covid 19 end.

I'm not making political statements; I don't want to prove a point.
But we owed to her and her carers, in her old age last place joint.

The dignity is all lost now, our love is plastic masks.
They hold her hand for me now, and not for me to ask.

But we must learn for next time, and I'm sure that it will come
To protect the ones like Edna, and not some smoking gun

I only write this out of love, and thanks as well to them
To the carers who give everything, and my guilt that leaves me numb.

Bruce, sit with me please.

18th May 2020

This a world with new opportunities and inevitably there are loads of companies offering a complete range of face masks, with home-made and posh ones, online designs and all.

News headlines

New measures have been deployed on trains and at stations amid fears that more people might use public transport to return to work in England this week. Train firms have operated reduced services due to coronavirus, but more frequent trains are now running. People are being encouraged to go back to work in England, but to only use public transport for essential journeys when they have no alternative

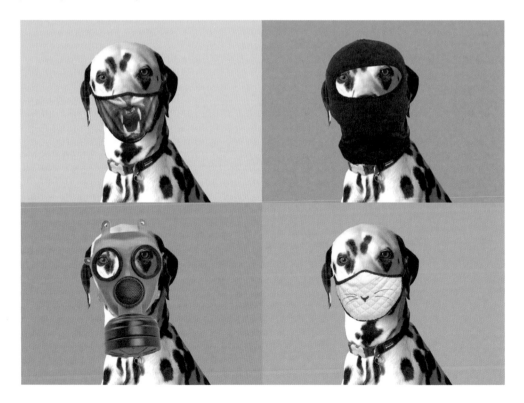

Get your face masks here

You just know it will happen, when we open the shops, the markets and shopping malls.
We won't be buying just scarves and gloves, it's fancy face masks for all.

Single colour, hygienic and plain as well and ones with furry dice.
Ones with zips so you can stick out your tongue, at anyone who is out with a cough.

And not wearing a face mask but plain old skin, and a mouth exposed to the air.
Get your face masks here, protect yourself and show the world that you care.

Of course, if you've money and designer dreams, Louis Vuitton or Marks and Sparks,
Big ones and small ones, ones made of jeans, as long as it designer marks.

But there will always be a face mask for me, at Poundland or Aldi too.
I'll buy in bulk, keep some in my car, in my favourite colour and hue.

I wonder if I can get some ones for my dog, just in case he wants to match mine.
So, when we're walking down the street, we look like a fashion line.

It's the new thing for summer, everyone will have one, of course it's also the rule.
So, wear your face masks and smile underneath, it will be the new world cool.

19th May 2020

The late Sam Cooke appeared to know what he was talking about when he wrote 'A change is gonna to come'. Sadly gone too soon, but my tribute to him is your daily virus poem today. Sing along…

News headlines

The number of people claiming unemployment benefit in the UK soared to 2.1 million last month, the first full month of the coronavirus lockdown. The total in April went up by 856,500, the Office for National Statistics (ONS) said. Separate ONS figures showed UK unemployment rose by 50,000 to 1.35 million in the three months to March.

A change is gonna come

We've all made changes to our lives, in our daily life routine.
Some are good, and some not so, like eating lots of beans.

But what will you do in the future? Will you change the way you are?
Will you stick with all the positives, as you get back in your car?

I, for one, are glad of some, simple household chores.
Satisfaction doing promised jobs, when I'm stuck behind my door.

Will we stick with talking to our friends? Will we stick with FaceTime too?
And perhaps when we are outside, change the way that I touch you.

Sam Cooke sang of coming change. Well, it's already here.
So, what we do is up to us as we drive and change the gear.

When life speeds up, back so fast, and stresses change from now.
Remember when time sat on your side and try and change somehow.

Sam knew what he was talking about in that little tent.

20th May 2020

Thank heavens we are good at queuing! Its impressive to see the discipline of the British and our stiff upper lip thingy. Now off to queue...

News headlines

Rolls-Royce has said it will cut 9,000 jobs and warned it will take "several years" for the airline industry to recover from the coronavirus pandemic. The firm, which makes engines for planes, said the reduction of nearly a fifth of its workforce would mainly affect its civil aerospace division. "This is not a crisis of our making but it is the crisis that we face and must deal with," boss Warren East said.

Queue

We are the best in the world at queuing, it's a British thing we do.
Now we live in world where's it compulsory, we even do it for the loo.

So, queuing for our shopping and not pushing to the front.
Queuing for the chemist, queuing not confront.

Soon well be queuing around the corner, down the road and cross the park.
We might be able to book our place, with the early morning lark.

So, as we get up in the morning, and pull the curtains wide.
We see our queue place ready, even though we're still inside.

It's a bit like queuing at Wimbledon; gosh! it's a shame that it's not on.
Back to queuing tactics, I hope it won't be long.

I hope I don't have to queue, when our walking out with Bruce.
I'm not sure he could do it; his discipline is loose.

I'll have a word with him and teach him what to do.
So, he can save my place for me, whilst I'm still in the loo.

Hang on Bruce, I'll be there soon.

21st May 2020

Whilst I have tried to write on a variety of subjects there is something consistent about Captain Tom that engages with all of us. And there is justice in the world recognising popular demand and so for the 3rd time.

News headlines

Captain Tom Moore said he was "overawed" on finding out he was to be awarded a knighthood for his fundraising efforts. Boris Johnson said he had provided the country with "a beacon of light through the fog of coronavirus". As an honorary colonel, his official title will be Captain Sir Thomas Moore under Ministry of Defence protocol.

Rejoice! Rejoice!

Rejoice! Rejoice! Let the bells ring out, we love a bit of good news.
We live in time of plague and strife, for most, for all, for few.

As I read the news, I cried out loud, and smiled from ear to ear.
I called my friends to share with them at this poignant time of year

It's not the sun, nor death rate falls, not petrol costs are low.
It's Captain Tom, the man we love and the knighthood now to show.

Captain Sir Thomas Moore rise up, you stand for all that's good.
Your life now shared for nations chest; we applaud you as we should.

This little man now 10 feet tall, represents the strength of man
Humble, warm and 'over the top', I'd follow him when I can.

In times when many waver, when days seem really hard.
His positivity is infectious, we draw the winning card.

Rejoice! Rejoice! for Captain Tom, I share my life with you.
I know you too feel proud inside, that's what we British do.

Let me explain Bruce.

22nd May 2020

We all need a holiday don't we and while there are many challenges to travel it is to the UK we are turning. Where will you go…

News headlines

Anyone arriving in the UK from abroad could be fined £1,000 if they fail to self-isolate for 14 days, the government is expected to announce. Under the plans, health officials would be able to carry out spot checks to check whether people were complying. The new rules, which will also apply to British people returning from abroad, are not expected to come into force until next month.

To the woods (or the beach)

I suspect the days of travel, on holidays abroad,
Are now thing of the past, no more the boulevard.

But I want to go somewhere, want to get out of here.
So now I'm allowed to move more, somewhere I can disappear.

Maybe I'll go to the forest, to wander on the trails.
Bruce exploring by my side; a dog walk never fails.

Can't do city breaks at all, and I for one don't mind,
I love the space of freedom, a holiday of a kind.

It's the beach that beckons lots of us, with sand upon our feet.
Listening to the waves break, on our towel, our sandy seat.

I'd quite like an ice cream, from the whippy van.
Close my eyes and daydream, do anything I can.

This might help the UK, local business back.
Yes, that's what I'll do this summer, and wander on the track.

Hope it stays sunny!

23rd May 2020

With many businesses struggling, now is a time to be innovative, and I asked Bruce for some ideas and this is one of them...

News headlines

The PM's top aide Dominic Cummings says he did the "right thing" by travelling 260 miles to be near relatives during the coronavirus lockdown - adding that he did not care what it looked like. Mr Cummings is facing calls to resign over the journey, which he made when his wife had Covid-19 symptoms. Downing Street said he wanted to ensure he had childcare if he got symptoms.

The stretch limo

Given the changes in all our lives, I was talking to Bruce today.
As I've no one else to chat with, you'll understand what I say.

This lockdown and what comes after, is likely to last for a time.
And ever the entrepreneurial dog, he proposed a new business line

We would buy an old stretched limo, paint it white with lots of spots.
We'd call it 'Dalmatian Driving', and this is what we've got.

A classy taxi service; your space to sit right down.
And yet keep your social distance, as with the rules of crown.

That way you can do your shopping, visit granny or the zoo.
All the time you'd have 2 metres, a limousine made for you.

We'd even have drinks and biscuits, served by Bruce sitting in the back.
Clearly, I'd do the driving, and he'd eat all the snacks.

It's fool proof I can tell you, apart from one small sign.
Unfortunately, that involves Bruce, he gets car sick all the time.

So, we've decided not to do it, and think up some more ideas.
If you have any thoughts please, not driving, hope that is clear.

Back to the drawing board Bruce!

24th May 2020

At first you don't notice, then over a period of weeks you realise that you have developed another friend – yourself; and someone talk too other than Bruce.

News headlines

When you talk to intensive care doctors across the UK, exhausted after weeks of dealing with the ravages of Covid-19, the phrase that emerges time after time is, "We've never seen anything like this before." They knew a new disease was coming, and they were expecting resources to be stretched by an unknown respiratory infection which had first appeared in China at the end of last year.

Talking to myself

Sadly, I've started talking to myself and I'm not doing very well.
I wait until my dog is asleep, so he doesn't tell!

All his friends in the park, that Mike is slightly mad.
I see them looking at me, and barking 'just how sad'.

But that is a sorry symptom, of living on your own.
With a dog that just won't talk to you, and it's just you two at home.

Oh yes - stick a treat in my hand, and he'll chat for flipping hours.
But when I want to discuss the virus, he goes off for a shower.

That's another annoying thing; he's using the bathroom more.
I had to wait for ages today, wet paw prints on the floor.

Anyway, back to talking, well, at least to myself
I wish I knew Dr Doolittle, to ask about my health.

And how I look for symptoms, in case I'm going crazy.
In these days we are locked away, the calendar all hazy.

Ha! I've just seen something funny, that's Bruce now fast asleep.
Talking away, well muttering, as he lays there in a heap.

So, it's not just me who's lost it; we're both the same, I guess.
At least we have each other. I wouldn't have anything less.

Let's talk about the weather Bruce!

25th May 2020

One day this will all be over hopefully, whatever the world becomes but at least you will be able to tell them…

News headlines

Online searches for cream teas and afternoon teas to be delivered have surged since the UK went into lockdown, search data has suggested. Afternoon tea treats topped the list of most increased searches for "delivery" queries in the UK, analysis of data from Google Trends showed. Other popular terms included TGI, Nando's, takeaways and cakes, as people looked for a "pick-me-up" treat.

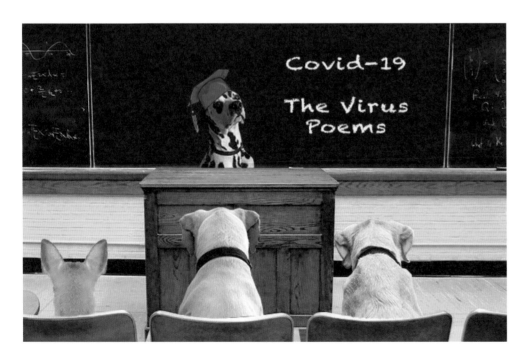

I was there

Many years from now, with grandchildren on the knee.
People will tell the story; what happened to you and me.

The pandemic of the twenties, like the crash a century before.
Will be taught in history classes, exams on spreading spores.

I hope the facts are accurate and not changed to blur and fool.
History always repeats itself; we know that is the rule.

Books will tell of Covid 19, graphs and maps as well.
There's bound to be professors, with degrees on virus hell.

Children will have some questions. What was clapping for?
Tell me about my relatives, tell me again once more.

So, sit them down and tell them, tell them how it was for you.
Be gentle on the tough bits, don't forget to hug them too.

Right now, it's not a syllabus, it's everyday life to bear.
This is our story for years to come. You can tell them 'I was there'!

You were there too Bruce.

26th May 2020

As time has drifted on for many of us self-isolating there is a sense of 'repeat' about our day. I don't know about you, but over this time I have lost a sense of reality and have to ask myself...

News headlines

All non-essential retailers will be able to reopen in England from 15 June, Boris Johnson has announced, as part of plans to further ease the lockdown. However, the move is contingent on progress in the fight against coronavirus, and retailers will have to adhere to new guidelines to protect shoppers and workers. Outdoor markets and car showrooms will be able to reopen from 1 June.

What day is it?

I've kind of lost all track of time, well, what I mean is days.
Not certain if it's the weekend or is it still Tuesday.

I don't get that Monday morning feeling, just on Monday's anymore.
I get it all the time now, in my daily schedule chore.

I do try to structure every day, but it doesn't matter much.
Each day is like the last one, with a later breakfast brunch.

Fortunately, I have my dog, and his day stays the same.
Feed me, love me, walk me, and then do it all again

But I'm looking forward to the time, when the week belongs to me
And each day is different from the last and the weekend sets me free

When once again I know the day, from the moment I get up.
In my diary I will book you in and re-join the 'normal' club.

Meanwhile time to walk the dog!

27th May 2020

I think it has been really tough on children and perhaps even harder now for parents as they go back to school. Not all though are going back on the 1st June. It may even be next term in September.

News headlines

"Local lockdowns" will be introduced to tackle regional outbreaks of c oronavirus in England in the future, the health secretary has said. Matt Hancock suggested restrictions will be introduced in areas with "flare-ups", but not others, as part of a system being put in place. He did not specify a timeframe, but said the measures will be part of the test, track and trace system.

Schools out for summer

When Alice Cooper sang his song, I wonder if he knew.
Just what that means to us right now, your children still with you.

The politicians have picked the day, for the schools to open soon.
Been a while, but it's a start, no more teaching zoom!

Except it's not for all of them, just little classes first.
The rest may have to wait a while, home teaching still enforced.

It's tough on them and tough on you, to keep them occupied.
And motivated, focussed too, while they're stuck inside.

The rise of mental health issues, affects the young ones too.
Slightly lost and asking why, puts pressure right on you.

I can't imagine just how long, before all the schools are open.
Before the noise of learning ones, of books and science potions.

So, when they come home from the day, with homework on the side.
Make them a drink and sit with them, education glorified!

Education, Education, Education - and that includes you Bruce!

28th May 2020

There still seems to be two worlds – the world where people are trying and the world of indifference. Watching the news item of an intensive care ward at a London hospital helps focus the mind…

News headlines

The number of US servicemen and women killed in Korea, Vietnam, Iraq and Afghanistan - over an aggregate 44 years of fighting is almost exactly the same as the number of Americans who've now lost their lives to coronavirus in just three months of America's war against the hidden enemy, as Donald Trump likes to refer to Covid-19.

Intensive care

I watched a thing on tv, about intensive care.
It made me realise so much, when life hangs on a prayer.

While outside people picnic, give up on distance too.
Lives hang in the balance, on ventilator glue.

They speeded up the footage, to show the busy ward.
The patient laying motionless, in a world that's quite absurd.

Bickering politics, arguments on trust.
All the time the docs and nurses, do everything they must.

And when the shift is over, emotions burst out loud.
Tired eyes of love and caring, but stopping's not allowed.

Repeat, repeat, tomorrow, to save the ones you can.
Hold hands of final moments, in the intensive caring plan.

You are unbelievable and thank you.

29th May 2020

As we move towards the new world and all the changes that are coming, they also include how we greet each other - as I found out when I stopped and chatted with a man I met when walking Bruce late one night...

News headlines

A police station in Minneapolis has been set alight during a third night of protests over the death of George Floyd. The unrest continued despite the governor of Minnesota ordering the deployment of hundreds of members of the National Guard to restore order. President Donald Trump said "thugs" were "dishonouring the memory" of George Floyd, 46, who died on Monday. Video showed him gasping for breath as a white policeman knelt on his neck.

Stay safe

It's the new farewell, as you say goodbye, no more, 'take care, see yay'
Instead we finish our little chats, with 'stay safe' and on your way.

I realised this as I walked down the road, and met a man standing there.
We stopped and spoke about this and that, about my funny hair

Anyway - when we'd done and came to part, I was about to say farewell.
But he beat me to it with 'stay safe' instead, so that's what I've got to tell.

You hear it on the news now, and from famous people too.
Graham Norton did it on Eurovision, Norway nil points to you.

Thank heavens it's that and not something else, like 'stay alert' or 'cheers'.
It's hard to be cheery all the time, with so much we have to fear.

Whatever you do, make sure you speak, to the stranger walking passed.
Even if it's a friendly wave, it's a simple little task.

I'm grateful for that chat I had, with the man I met in the lane.
And so, I say to all of you, 'stay safe' once more again.

You cannot say it enough - stay safe!

30th May 2020

As the Virus poems draw to a close - for now - I had to take a brief moment to acknowledge my amazing friend who has been with me for the whole journey and will still be here if I write a duff poem…

News headlines

The UK has experienced its sunniest spring since records began and is set to be the driest May on record for some parts of UK. The UK spent much of spring in lockdown due to the coronavirus pandemic, but thousands flocked to beaches last week to enjoy the sun following a slight easing of restrictions in England.

My dog Bruce

This has been quite a journey, and mostly on my own.
Except of course I've got Bruce, turns my flat into a home.

I don't think I could have made it, without him by my side.
There's been times when I've just sat there, and without him would have cried.

If you've a dog, you'll know well, just what he means to me.
I love my spotty crazy friend; he helps to set me free.

Walking him's a pleasure, morning, night or afternoon.
He's figured in the pictures, the sketches and cartoons

His love is unconditional, and mine is back to him.
It's Mike and Bruce forever, without him life is grim.

So, when I write my poems, I include him on the way.
I hope he makes you laugh as well and brightens up your day.

In fact, the book I'll publish, will credit him as well.
'Virus Poems' from Mike Bourton, but Bruce will help them sell!

Who's a good boy!

31st May 2020

I feel a little sad about finishing but I had to stop at some point and so, on the 31st May, that time has come. I will see you all I am sure and so for now, thank you everyone and let's hope that the change is going to come for the better. Lets hope so.

News headlines

Vulnerable people in England who have been asked to remain at home since the coronavirus lockdown began will be able to go outdoors again from Monday. Those with families will be able to go out once a day with members of their household. People living alone can meet one other person from another household while maintaining social distancing.

The last virus poem

My gosh! This has been a journey, and it's not quite over yet.
But this is my last poem, my 'Virus Poem' set.

We've been a distance together, social distance too.
Hoarders and key workers, Donald, Boris, you.

We had 'love when we went shopping', cut my hair in funny ways.
Bruce looked for a police job, all the time we had to stay.

Inside with our baked beans, with the clock just ticking by.
Personal space a daily challenge, personal hygiene my oh my!

I wrote about the people, just doing jobs for us.
I wrote about thing virtual and things we could discuss.

And don't forget that numbers, are people, not just graphs.
It really was a tough time, though sometimes we had a laugh.

I don't know what's going to happen, and if you do please tell.
For you and me are real now, I only wish you well.

Thank you for being there with me, for likes and comments too.
Now I know just what I want, I still want hugs with you.

Might be a while though won't it!

Whilst 'The Virus Poems' go up to the 31st May 2020 this is obviously not the end of the story. No one really knows what will happen in the months and years to come. I hope not to be writing another set of virus poems and would rather write about something different. However, I am eternally grateful for many aspects of this journey and how it has allowed me to connect with so many people, albeit virtually. I have made friends, sharing similar experiences along the way. And of course, none of this would have been possible with out my faithful dog, Bruce.

Living in isolation is a challenge that has affected us in so many ways – both the young and old, but if we can ensure we remember just some of the journey and how we coped then we can move forward with some optimism. How we applauded the wonderful people who worked tirelessly, supporting those in need, and sometimes were the last hand to be held.

This is not a period to be triumphed – it is a time to be remembered as we move into whatever the world offers us now.

I wish you all the best fortune for tomorrow.